HAPPY TRAILS 1

GRAMMAR
INTERNATIONAL EDITION

Erika Antorka

Contents

	Grammar	Page
Unit 1	A/An, Personal Pronouns	4
Unit 2	To be	6
Unit 3	Plurals (-s)	12
Unit 4	This is/That is, These/Those are, What is/are …?	14
Review 1	Units 1-4	18
Unit 5	There is, There are, How many …?	20
Unit 6	A/An/The	26
Unit 7	Have got	28
Unit 8	Possessive 's, Possessive adjectives	34
Review 2	Units 5-8	36

Contents

	Grammar	Page
Unit 9	Can	38
Unit 10	Present Continuous, What ... doing?	42
Unit 11	Imperative, Let's	50
Unit 12	Plurals (-es, -ies, irregulars)	54
Review 3	Units 9-12	58
Unit 13	Some and Any	60
Unit 14	Prepositions of place, Where is ...?/Where are ...?	62
Unit 15	Present Simple	66
Unit 16	Prepositions of time, What ... + prepositions of time, Question words	74
Review 4	Units 13-16	78
Wordlist		80
Tests		84

A/An, Personal Pronouns

"A fly. No, an elephant!"

A/An

We put **a** before a word to talk about one person, animal or thing.

If the word begins with **a**, **e**, **i**, **o** or **u**, then we use **an**.

A Circle.

1. (a) / an panda
2. a / an song
3. a / an octopus
4. a / an girl
5. a / an quilt
6. a / an egg

B Write a or an.

1. _an_ elephant
2. ____ dog
3. ____ car
4. ____ insect
5. ____ baby
6. ____ fox

Speaking

"An ant!"

Say.

Unit 1

Personal pronouns

We use these words (personal pronouns) to show who someone is or who is doing something.

I
you
he
she
it
we
you
they

She is a nice girl.
It's a blue pencil.

C Write.

he
he
it
me
she
they
~~we~~

D Write.

~~boy~~	mum
car	pencil
dad	sister
Emily	spider
girl	Tom
king	worm

he	she	it
boy	_____	_____
_____	_____	_____
_____	_____	_____
_____	_____	_____

5

To be

To be – affirmative

We use the verb **to be** to say who a person is or what a thing is. When we speak, we usually use the short form.

I **am**   I**'m**
you **are**   you**'re**
he **is**   he**'s**
she **is**   she**'s**
it **is**   it**'s**
we **are**   we**'re**
you **are**   you**'re**
they **are**   they**'re**

Am, **are** and **is** go after the personal pronouns (**I**, **you**, **we**, **they** etc) or after the name of a person, animal or thing.

Note
In English we always use personal pronouns with verbs. We must say, for example, **we are**.

I **am** John.
Penny **is** a girl.
A frog **is** green.
Robots **are** fantastic!

A Match and colour.

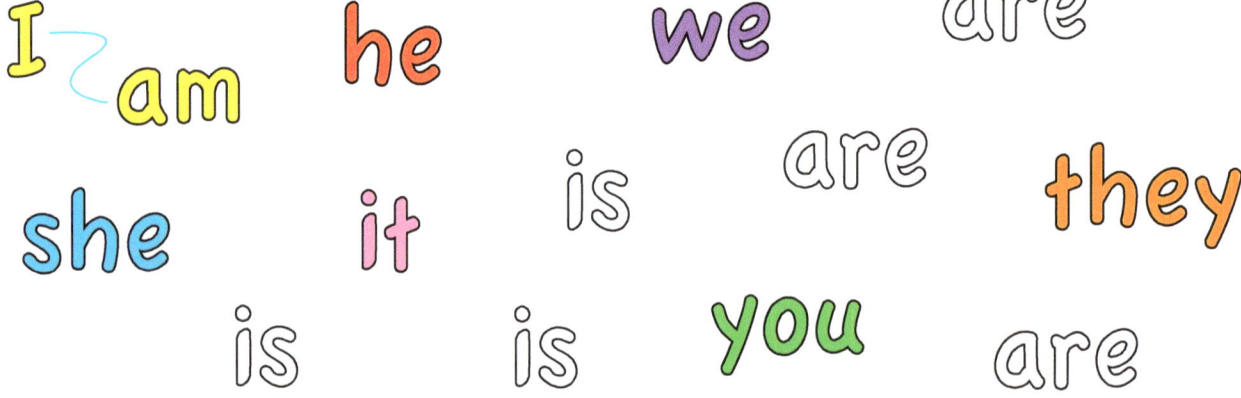

Unit 2

B Circle.

1 Africa is / are cool.
2 I am / is seven.
3 Mia is / am a meerkat.
4 Ty, Mia and Leo is / are friends.
5 We are / am pupils.
6 You are / is fantastic!
7 They are / is babies.
8 It am / is an elephant.

C Write am, are or is.

My name (1) __is__ Ryan.
I (2) _____ eight. I'm from England.
My sister (3) _____ six. Look! My
mum and dad (4) _____ in the
photo too. They (5) _____ cool!
Grandma (6) _____ happy.
Grandpa (7) _____ happy too. We
(8) _____ all happy.

Say.

I'm Matilda. I'm eight. I'm from England. My sister is Sabrina. She's five. My mum and dad are nice.

It isn't a toy. It's a camera!

To be – negative

We put **not** after **am**, **are** and **is** to say who a person isn't or what a thing isn't. When we speak, we usually use the short form.

I **am not**   I**'m not**
you **are not**   you **aren't**
he **is not**   he **isn't**
she **is not**   she **isn't**
it **is not**   it **isn't**
we **are not**   we **aren't**
you **are not**   you **aren't**
they **are not**   they **aren't**

You **aren't** funny.
They **aren't** short.

D   Write 'm not, isn't or aren't.

1   It ___isn't___ a robot.

2   He _____ Grandpa!

3   They _____ teddy bears.

4   We _____ best friends.

5   It _____ an octopus.

6   I _____ a boy.

Unit 2

E **Write.**

~~aren't~~   aren't   isn't   isn't   isn't   'm not

1 The cakes ___aren't___ blue. They're brown.
2 It _____ an ant. It's a worm.
3 They _____ igloos. They're balls.
4 She's tall. She _____ short.
5 I _____ nine. I'm ten.
6 He's from Africa. He _____ from England.

F **Circle.**

1 They ___ tall.
   a aren't
   b are

5 We ___ brothers.
   a aren't
   b are

2 He ___ happy.
   a is
   b isn't

6 It ___ fun!
   a is
   b isn't

3 I ___ a spider!
   a 'm not
   b am

7 You ___ funny.
   a are
   b aren't

4 She ___ a baby.
   a isn't
   b is

8 We ___ cool.
   a are
   b aren't

To be – question and short answer

To ask questions with **to be** we put **am**, **are** or **is** at the beginning of the question. We can give short answers with **Yes** or **No**, the person and **am**, **are** or **is**.

Am I …?
Are you …?
Is he …?
Is she …?
Is it …?
Are we …?
Are you …?
Are they …?

Are you a king?
Yes, I **am**. / No, I'm **not**.

Are they pencils?
Yes, they **are**. / No, they **aren't**.

G Match.

1  Is it a camera?   a Yes, he is.

2  Is he happy?   b No, it isn't.

3  Are they sisters?   c Yes, it is.

4  Are they giraffes?   d No, they aren't.

5  Is it a birthday cake? e Yes, they are.

Unit 2

H Write **Am**, **Are** or **Is**.

1 __Is__ the toy small?
2 _____ the cakes yummy?
3 _____ Emily happy?
4 _____ I cool?

5 _____ you OK?
6 _____ we tall?
7 _____ it a leopard?
8 _____ she your mum?

I Write.

1  Are you ten?
Yes, I am.

2  Is she short?
_____

3  Is it a fox?
_____

4  Are they cakes?
_____

5  Are we friends?
_____

6  Is he a hunter?
_____

Speaking

Say.

Is it small? — No, it isn't.
Is it tall? — Yes, it is.
Is it a giraffe? — Yes, it is.

Plurals -s

One banana and three monkeys!

Plurals -s

To talk about more than one person, animal or thing, we usually add **-s** at the end of the word.

one sister → four sister**s**
one insect → two insect**s**

A Circle.

1 (hat) / hats   2 insects / insect   3 candles / candle

4 photo / photos   5 house / houses   6 brother / brothers

B Circle and write.

eme(lephants)anafsyyoumonkeysandamonkeyisantsweantnaelephant

elephants

12

Unit 3

C Write.

1
one ball   seven balls

3
one camera   _____

2
one bird   _____

4
one frog   _____

Speaking

Three dogs!

Say.

This is/That is, These are/Those are, What is …?/What are …?

This is Mum and that's Dad.

This is/That is

We use **This** to point to a person, animal or thing which is near us. We use **That** to point to a person, animal or thing which is far away from us.

This is an animal.
That is a flower.

Note
There is a short form: **That is** → **That's**

A Circle.

1 (This) / That is a rabbit.
   This / (That) is a cat.

2 This / That is a lion.
   This / That is a monkey.

3 This / That is a dolphin.
   This / That is a whale.

4 This / That is a sandwich.
   This / That is cake.

5 This / That is a bird.
   This / That is a dog.

6 This / That is a computer game.
   This / That is a toy.

Unit 4

These oranges are yummy! Those bees are hungry!

These are/Those are

To point to more than one person, animal or thing that is near us we use **These**. We use the word **Those** if they are far away from us.

These are animals.
Those are flowers.

B Write **these** or **those**.

1

These are meerkats and _those_ are monkeys.

3

_____ cakes are yummy but _____ cakes aren't nice.

2

_____ are big eggs and _____ are small eggs.

4

_____ are ants and _____ are spiders.

C Circle.

1 That / (Those) are teddy bears.
2 This / These are flowers.
3 This / Those is an ostrich.
4 That / Those are baby lions.
5 This / These is a tree.
6 That / Those is a whale.

What's that?

It's a ... bird?!?

What is ...?/What are ...?

We use **What** to ask about actions, animals, things, etc. To answer questions with **What ...?** we use **It's** for one thing and **They're** for many things.

What is this?   **It's** a dolphin.
What is that?   **It's** a tree.
What are these?   **They're** toys.
What are those?   **They're** hats.

Note
There is a short form: **What is ...?** → **What's ...?**

D Choose and write.

~~It's~~   It's   It's   They're
They're   They're

an igloo   a robot   ~~a shark~~
dolphins   penguins   skateboards

1 What's that?
   It's a shark.

4 What's this?
   _____

2 What are these?
   _____

5 What are those?
   _____

3 What are those?
   _____

6 What's that?
   _____

Unit 4

E Write What's or What are and match.

1 __What's__ this? a They're worms.

2 _____ these? b It's a teddy bear.

3 _____ that? c It's a car.

4 _____ that? d They're ants.

5 _____ those? e It's a lion.

Speaking

Say.

Review 1 (Units 1-4)

A Write.

1 two ____lions____

2 three _____

3 five _____

4 seven _____

5 eight _____

6 ten _____

B Write.

egg
elephant
~~fly~~
friend
insect
ostrich
photo
skateboard

a	an
fly	_____
_____	_____
_____	_____
_____	_____

C Write am, are or is.

~~am~~   are   are   are   is   is

1 I ___am___ Liz.

2 He _____ my brother.

3 We _____ friends.

4 They _____ boys.

5 It _____ an egg.

6 You _____ tall!

Review 1

D Circle.

1 She aren't / (isn't) seven.
2 We aren't / 'm not sad.
3 It aren't / isn't green.
4 I 'm not / aren't a boy!
5 They isn't / aren't cool!
6 You aren't / isn't a baby!

E Write.

1 ___Is___ it small?
  Yes, it __is__ .
2 _____ they short?
  No, they _____ .
3 _____ she happy?
  No, she _____ .
4 _____ he your dad?
  Yes, he _____ .
5 _____ you brothers?
  No, we _____ .

F Circle and write.

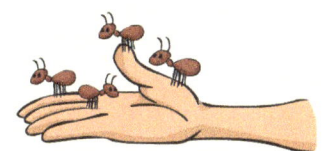

1 What are (these) / those?
  __They're__ ants.

2 What are these / those?
  _____ birds.

3 What's this / that?
  _____ a snake.

4 What's this / that?
  _____ a mountain.

5 What's this / that?
  _____ a lizard.

6 What are these / those?
  _____ lemons.

There is/There are and How many ...?

There is/There are

We use **There is** (for one thing) to say what exists. But we use **There are** for more than one thing.

There is a pen on the book.
There are photos on the desk.

Note
There is a short form: **There is** → **There's**

A Write.

	There is	There are
~~ants~~	a lion	ants
birds		
helicopter		
~~lion~~		
lizard		
rabbits		
snake		
spiders		

Unit 5

B Circle. Then write Yes or No.

1 (There are) / There is meerkats in Africa.   Yes
2 There's / There are a spider in my bag.   _____
3 There are / There's a giraffe in the car.   _____
4 There's / There are sharks in that helicopter.   _____
5 There's / There are dolphins in the sea.   _____
6 There's / There are a teacher in the classroom.   _____
7 There are / There's lions in the school.   _____
8 There's / There are a bear in the cake.   _____
9 There are / There's boys and girls in my class.   _____
10 There are / There's drawings at our school.   _____

C Write There is or There are and draw.

A picnic! (1) __There are__ crisps. (2) _____ six green apples, (3) _____ eight sandwiches and (4) _____ a big bottle of lemonade. Yummy, (5) _____ a big pink cake. Oh no! (6) _____ three spiders too.

There isn't a pencil. There aren't any pens, but there are spiders!

There isn't/There aren't

We put **n't** (**not**) after **There is** and **There are** to say that there isn't a person, animal or thing.

There isn't a penguin in the classroom.

There aren't any monkeys in the tree.

D Circle.

1 There **isn't** / aren't a king in England.
2 There isn't / aren't twenty pencils in the box.
3 There isn't / aren't a snake in the tree.
4 There isn't / aren't elephants in Australia.
5 There isn't / aren't a photo in my bag.
6 There isn't / aren't a song in this unit.

E Write.

1 There's one teacher in the classroom. (two teachers)
   There aren't two teachers in the classroom.

2 There's a spider on the desk. (an ant)
   _____

3 There are ten toys in my bedroom. (fifteen toys)
   _____

4 There's a penguin in the igloo. (lion)
   _____

5 There's a yo-yo in my bag. (a present)
   _____

6 There's a bird in the tree. (flowers)
   _____

Unit 5

F Tick (✓) or cross (✗).

1 There isn't a teacher.   ✓
2 There aren't any boys.   ____
3 There isn't a computer.   ____
4 There aren't six girls.   ____
5 There isn't a board.   ____
6 There aren't any notebooks. ____
7 There aren't five pupils. ____
8 There aren't any mums and dads. ____

Speaking

There isn't a beach.

Say.

- ~~beach~~
- blue and yellow umbrellas
- blue hat
- blue houses
- boys
- car
- cat
- dog
- flowers
- girls
- trees
- yellow houses

23

Is there ...?/Are there ...? and short answer

To ask if there is a person, animal or thing, we put **is** or **are** at the beginning of the question. We can give short answers with **Yes, there is / are** or **No, there isn't / aren't**.

Is there an apple on the book?
Yes, **there is**. / No, **there isn't**.

Are there ten boys in your class?
Yes, **there are**. / No, **there aren't**.

G **Write about your school.**

1 ? / a cat / there / is
   Is there a cat?
   No, there isn't.

2 ? / is / a big tree / there

3 ? / girls / are / there

4 ? / toys / are / there

5 ? / there / is / a bus

6 ? / insects / there / are

7 ? / there / is / a helicopter

8 ? / are / drawings / there

24

Unit 5

How many ...?

To ask the number of things a person has got, or the number of people, animals or things there are, we use **How many ...?**. We answer with **There is** / **There are**.

How many cars are there?
There are five cars.

Speaking

How many balls are there?

There are three balls.

Say.

6 A/An/The

There's a wave. The wave is really big!

A/An/The

We use **a** and **an** to talk about one person, animal or thing. We use **the** instead of **a/an** to talk about a specific person, animal or thing, or to talk about it, or them, again.

Look! **A** helicopter. **The** helicopter is big.

We also use **the** to talk about something which is unique, for example *the sky, the moon, the sun*.

The sun is yellow.
The sky is blue.

A Write **a**, **an** or **the**.

1 __an__ ant

2 _____ sun

3 _____ egg

4 _____ book

5 _____ sky

6 _____ apple

7 _____ computer

8 _____ umbrella

9 _____ moon

10 _____ helicopter

Unit 6

B **Circle.**

1 **The** / A sun is yellow.
2 There's a / the big tree outside.
3 There's the / a helicopter in the / a sky.
4 Is this a / the blue pen?
5 That's a / an egg.
6 Look! It's the / a moon.

C **Write a, an, or the.**

1 There isn't ___a___ bird in ___the___ tree.
2 There are waves in _____ sea. _____ waves are big.
3 That's _____ funny hat!
4 There's _____ elephant in the garden! _____ elephant is hungry.
5 _____ sun isn't purple. It's yellow!
6 That isn't _____ aeroplane. It's _____ helicopter.

D **Write a, an, or the. Then draw and colour.**

In my bedroom, there is (1) ___a___ green desk and (2) _____ blue chair. On (3) _____ desk, there is (4) _____ pen and two pencils. (5) _____ pen is black and (6) _____ pencils are red and orange. There is (7) _____ notebook and two books. (8) _____ notebook is brown and (9) _____ books are yellow. There is (10) _____ grey computer too.

7 Have got

Have got – affirmative

We use **have got** to say that a thing belongs to a person or to describe a person or thing. When we speak, we usually use the short form.

I **have got**	I**'ve got**
you **have got**	you**'ve got**
he **has got**	he**'s got**
she **has got**	she**'s got**
it **has got**	it**'s got**
we **have got**	we**'ve got**
you **have got**	you**'ve got**
they **have got**	they**'ve got**

Have got and **has got** go after the personal pronouns (**I**, **you**, **he**, **she**, **it**, **we**, **they**) and after the name of a person, animal or thing.

I**'ve got** two brothers.
Paul**'s got** a computer.
The lion**'s got** a long tail.
The robot **has got** yellow eyes.

A Write.

1 You have got a computer.   ___You've got___ a computer.
2 He has got a funny cat.   _____ a funny cat.
3 It has got a long tail.   _____ a long tail.
4 They have got red pens.   _____ red pens.
5 You have got a brother.   _____ a brother.
6 She has got two rabbits.   _____ two rabbits.
7 We have got teddy bears.   _____ teddy bears.
8 I have got a camera.   _____ a camera.

Unit 7

B Write **have got** or **has got**.

1 Sally ___has got___ ten toes.
2 Birds _____ two legs.
3 This kangaroo _____ big ears.
4 I _____ a red nose.
5 My sister _____ wet hair.
6 We _____ a ball.

C Circle.

I (1) 's got / **'ve got** three cats. They (2) 's got / 've got black noses. This is Mickey. Mickey (3) 've got / 's got sad eyes, but he's happy!

This is a tarantula spider. It (4) 've got / 's got eight legs. It (5) 's got / 've got hair. These spiders (6) has got / have got big teeth too.

Speaking

Draw and say.

It's got green hair. It's got three eyes and a funny hat.

Have got – negative

We put the word **not** after **have** / **has** to make the negative form. When we speak, we usually use the short form.

I **have not got**
you **have not got**
he **has not got**
she **has not got**
it **has not got**
we **have not got**
you **have not got**
they **have not got**

I **haven't got**
you **haven't got**
he **hasn't got**
she **hasn't got**
it **hasn't got**
we **haven't got**
you **haven't got**
they **haven't got**

I **haven't got** a dog.
They **haven't got** a sister.

D   **Write haven't got or hasn't got.**

1. Ants have got six legs. They ___haven't got___ eight legs.
2. Tom has got a cat. He _____ a dog.
3. You've got a pencil. You _____ a pen.
4. Mum's got a small car. She _____ a big car.
5. We've got skateboards. We _____ bicycles.
6. The elephant has got a long nose. It _____ a long tail.
7. I've got a thin cat. I _____ a fat cat.
8. John and Kate have got a pet lizard. They _____ a pet snake.

Unit 7

E **Circle.**

1 Mia and Ty have got / haven't got surfboards.
2 Leo hasn't got / has got a surfboard.
3 They 've got / haven't got a picnic.
4 Mia 's got / hasn't got a ball.
5 They haven't got / 've got a camera.
6 Leo 's got / hasn't got a hat.
7 They haven't got / 've got a beach umbrella.
8 Ty 's got / hasn't got the cake.

F **Write have got or haven't got.**

Hi, I'm Mary. This is my bag. My bag is yellow! I (1) ___have got___ a rubber and a ruler in my bag. I (2) _____ a book but I (3) _____ two notebooks. I (4) _____ three pencils too. I (5) _____ a present, but I (6) _____ an apple for my teacher.

Have got – question and short answer

We put **have** or **has** at the beginning of a question to ask if a person has got a thing. We can give short answers with **Yes** or **No**, the person and **have** / **has** or **haven't** / **hasn't**.

Have I **got** ...? Yes, I **have**. / No, I **haven't**.
Have you **got** ...? Yes, you **have**. / No, you **haven't**.
Has he **got** ...? Yes, he **has**. / No, he **hasn't**.
Has she **got** ...? Yes, she **has**. / No, she **hasn't**.
Has it **got** ...? Yes, it **has**. / No, it **hasn't**.
Have we **got** ...? Yes, we **have**. / No, we **haven't**.
Have you **got** ...? Yes, you **have**. / No, you **haven't**.
Have they **got** ...? Yes, they **have**. / No, they **haven't**.

Has Tom **got** a car?
Yes, he **has**. / No, he **hasn't**.

Have you **got** a TV?
Yes, we **have**. / No, we **haven't**.

Note

When **have** is in the question, we answer with **have** or **haven't**, and when **has** is in the question we answer with **has** or **hasn't**. We don't use **got** in short answers.

G Write **Have** or **Has** and match.

1 _Has_ Annie got flippers? a No, I haven't.
2 _____ rabbits got long ears? b Yes, she has.
3 _____ Ty got a camera? c Yes, he has.
4 _____ a snake got legs? d No, it hasn't.
5 _____ you got a big nose? e Yes, they have.

Unit 7

H Write.

Leglong

Strengo

1 Has Leglong got big eyes?   Yes, she has.
2 Has Strengo got two arms?   _____
3 Has Strengo got one leg?   _____
4 Have they got black hair?   _____
5 Has Leglong got long legs?   _____
6 Has Strengo got fourteen fingers?   _____

Speaking

Have you got a pencil?

Yes, I have.

Say.

8 Possessive 's, Possessive Adjectives

Possessive 's

We put **'s** after the name of a person to show who a thing belongs to.

It's **Kathy's** mobile phone.
They're **Billy's** shoes.

We can also put **'s** after a person (**I**, **you**, **he**, etc) or animal to show who owns something.

It's **dad's** shirt.
They're the **dog's** toys.

A Write.

1 They're ___Todd's___ flippers.
2 It's _____ hat.
3 It's _____ dress.
4 It's _____ computer game.
5 They're _____ books.
6 They're _____ shoes.
7 It's _____ mask.
8 It's _____ skateboard.
9 It's _____ ball.

Unit 8

Possessive adjectives

We can use these words (possessive adjectives) to show whose something is.

my   our
your   your
his   their
her
its

Note

Possessive adjectives always go before the noun.

It's *her* mask.

Don't confuse *it's* = *it is* with the possessive adjective *its*.

B Match and colour.

he — her — his   it   I

she   their   its   we

they   our   your   my   you

C Write.

1 Look at that dog! ____Its____ tail is pink.
2 They're funny cats. _____ ears are small.
3 We're sisters. _____ dresses are green.
4 I'm happy. _____ apple is yummy.
5 Tom is sad. _____ milk is cold.
6 Sally is cool. _____ jeans are new.
7 You're wet! _____ umbrella is old.
8 That's an elephant. _____ nose is long.

Review 2 (Units 5-8)

A Circle.

1 (There are) / There aren't seven candles.

2 There isn't / There is a girl.

3 There are / There aren't ten notebooks.

4 There isn't / There is a teddy bear.

5 There are / There aren't three monkeys.

6 There is / There isn't a pencil.

B Write have got, has got, haven't got or hasn't got.

1 Elephants ____have got____ big ears.
2 Giraffes _____ short legs.
3 My baby sister _____ a car.
4 My schoolbag _____ books and pencils in it.
5 A snake _____ any hands.

C Write.

1 ___Has___ Trek got a camera?   Yes, ___he has___.
2 _____ spiders got eight legs?   Yes, _____.
3 _____ your dog got a black nose? Yes, _____.
4 _____ a fish got legs?   No, _____.
5 _____ cats got fingers?   No, _____.

D Write.

ant	moon
arm	photo
~~computer~~	sea
desk	sun
elephant	

a	an	the
computer		

Review 2

E **Write about your bedroom.**

1. __Is there__ a bed?   Yes, there is.
2. _____ any toys?   _____
3. _____ a computer?   _____
4. _____ any trees?   _____
5. _____ a board?   _____
6. _____ any books?   _____

F **Write How many and count.**

1. __How many__ rulers are there?
   There are three rulers.
2. _____ books are there?
   _____
3. _____ eggs are there?
   _____
4. _____ yo-yos are there?
   _____
5. _____ apples are there?
   _____
6. _____ pencils are there?
   _____

G **Write.**

1. __Paul's__ notebook
2. _____ book
3. _____ pen
4. _____ pencil
5. _____ rubber

H **Write.**

| her   his   its   my   ~~our~~   their   your |

1. We put _____our_____ books in the bookcase.
2. _____ name is Angela. What's _____ name?
3. Laura has got a brother. _____ name is Brandon.
4. Has Helen got a computer in _____ bedroom?
5. This is a rabbit. _____ ears are big.
6. The children are in _____ classroom.

37

Can

"I can dance the samba!"

Can – affirmative

We use the word **can** and a verb to say what we are able to do.

I **can sing**.
You **can sing**.
He **can sing**.
She **can sing**.
It **can sing**.
We **can sing**.
You **can sing**.
They **can sing**.

A Tick (✓) or cross (✗).

1 Snakes can run. ✗
2 Parrots can speak. ☐
3 Koalas can sing. ☐
4 Kangaroos can jump. ☐
5 Dancers can dance. ☐
6 Dolphins can read. ☐

B Write.

dance   ~~jump~~   read   run   sing   swim

1  He ___can jump___ .

2  She _____ .

3  They _____ .

4  They _____ .

5  He _____ .

6  They _____ .

Can – negative

We use **cannot** or **can't** to say what we are not able to do. We usually use the short form.

I **cannot sing**.
You **cannot sing**.
He **cannot sing**.
She **cannot sing**.
It **cannot sing**.
We **cannot sing**.
You **cannot sing**.
They **cannot sing**.

I **can't sing**.
You **can't sing**.
He **can't sing**.
She **can't sing**.
It **can't sing**.
We **can't sing**.
You **can't sing**.
They **can't sing**.

C **Circle.**

1 Bears (can) / can't run but they can / (can't) read.
2 An octopus can / can't swim but it can / can't speak.
3 Dolphins can / can't play with a ball but they can / can't sit down.
4 A leopard can / can't dance but it can / can't run.

D **Write can or can't.**

1  My teacher ___can___ read but she ___can't___ draw.

2  My dog _____ jump but it _____ swim.

3  Tara _____ dance but she _____ sing.

4  My brother _____ speak but he _____ walk.

Can – question and short answer

We put **Can** at the beginning of a question to ask if a person is able to do an action. We answer with **Yes** or **No**, the person and **can** or **can't**.

Can I **sing**?	Yes, I **can**. / No, I **can't**.
Can you **sing**?	Yes, you **can**. / No, you **can't**.
Can he **sing**?	Yes, he **can**. / No, he **can't**.
Can she **sing**?	Yes, she **can**. / No, she **can't**.
Can it **sing**?	Yes, it **can**. / No, it **can't**.
Can we **sing**?	Yes, we **can**. / No, we **can't**.
Can you **sing**?	Yes, you **can**. / No, you **can't**.
Can they **sing**?	Yes, they **can**. / No, they **can't**.

E   Match.

1. Can a lion play the guitar?
2. Can Donald and Kelly play tennis?
3. Can Frank sing?
4. Can a dolphin swim?
5. Can you read?
6. Can Lucy dance?

a   No, it can't.
b   Yes, he can.
c   No, they can't.
d   Yes, she can.
e   Yes, I can.
f   Yes, it can.

F   Write about you.

1. Can you play the drums?   No, I can't.
2. Can your mum jump?   _____
3. Can your dad swim?   _____
4. Can you play volleyball?   _____
5. Can you dance?   _____
6. Can your teacher play the guitar? _____

Unit 9

G Write.

1 ? / Sam / can / read ✗
   Can Sam read?
   No, he can't.

2 ? / the boys / jump / can ✓

3 ? / swim / Kim / can ✗

4 ? / dance / can / your friends ✓

5 ? / the piano / play / can / Harry ✗

6 ? / play / the drums / can / Kathy ✓

Can parrots walk? Yes, they can.

Say.

	Parrots	Snakes
walk	✓	✗
fly	✓	✗
climb	✓	✓
swim	✗	✓
eat frogs	✗	✓

Present Continuous, What ... doing?

Present Continuous – affirmative

To talk about an action which is happening now, we use the **Present Continuous**. We form this tense with **am** / **are** / **is** + verb + **-ing**.

When we speak, we usually use the short form.

I **am** cook**ing**.	I**'m** cook**ing**.
You **are** cook**ing**.	You**'re** cook**ing**.
He **is** cook**ing**.	He**'s** cook**ing**.
She **is** cook**ing**.	She**'s** cook**ing**.
It **is** cook**ing**.	It**'s** cook**ing**.
We **are** cook**ing**.	We**'re** cook**ing**.
You **are** cook**ing**.	You**'re** cook**ing**.
They **are** cook**ing**.	They**'re** cook**ing**.

Note
When the verb ends in **-e**, we drop the **-e** before adding **-ing**.

dance	They're danc**ing**.
write	We're writ**ing**.

When the verb has got only one syllable and ends in **consonant-vowel-consonant**, we double the consonant at the end of the verb.

sit	She's sit**ting**.

Unit 10

A Write.

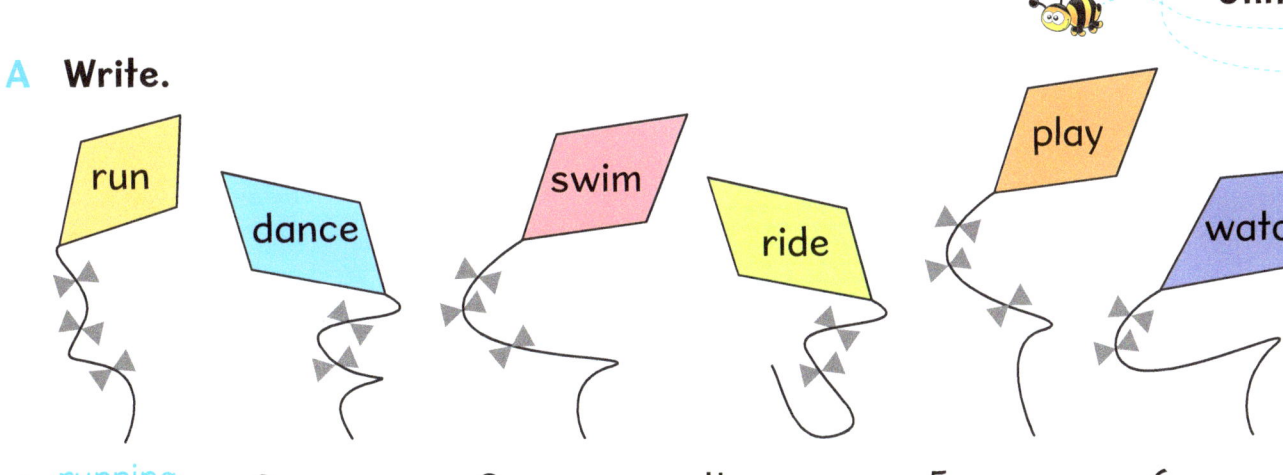

1 running   2 _____   3 _____   4 _____   5 _____   6 _____

B Match.

   1   She's playing a game.   4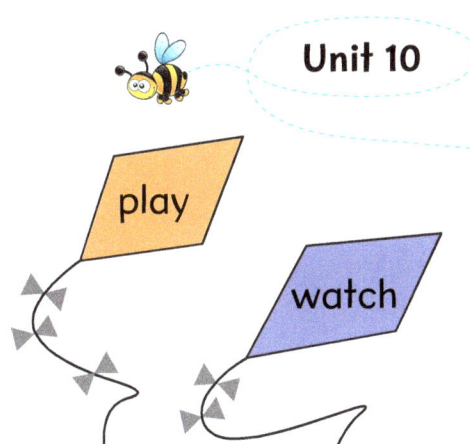

                       He's watching TV.

                       They're riding their bikes.   5

         2   You're reading!

                       It's eating.   6

         3   We're dancing.

C Write.

1 They are reading.
   They're reading.

2 He is sitting.

3 We are singing.

4 I am writing.

5 You are watching TV.

6 It is running.

7 She is sleeping.

8 They are playing tennis.

D **Write.**

eat
listen
play
~~read~~
sleep
watch

1 Grandpa ___is reading___ a book.
2 Tom and Lucy _____ a game.
3 Dad _____ TV.
4 The cat _____ on the floor.
5 Mum and Grandma _____ apples.
6 Meg _____ to music.

E **Write and colour.**

This is circus school. The animals (1) ___are having___ (have) fun. The elephant (2) _____ (play) a pink piano. The zebra and the lion (3) _____ (play) yellow drums and a purple guitar. The giraffe (4) _____ (ride) a red bike. The meerkat (5) _____ (sit) on its head. It (6) _____ (listen) to the music. The ostriches (7) _____ (dance). They have got orange hats and they (8) _____ (wear) blue socks.

Unit 10

Present Continuous – negative

We use the **Present Continuous** with **not** after **am**, **are**, **is** to say that a person is not doing an action now. When we speak, we usually use the short form.

I **am not** cook**ing**.   I**'m not** cook**ing**.
You **are not** cook**ing**.   You **aren't** cook**ing**.
He **is not** cook**ing**.   He **isn't** cook**ing**.
She **is not** cook**ing**.   She **isn't** cook**ing**.
It **is not** cook**ing**.   It **isn't** cook**ing**.
We **are not** cook**ing**.   We **aren't** cook**ing**.
You **are not** cook**ing**.   You **aren't** cook**ing**.
They **are not** cook**ing**.   They **aren't** cook**ing**.

F **Circle.**

1
It (isn't) / aren't sleeping.

2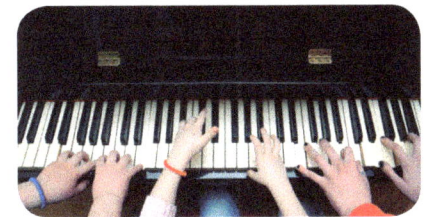
They isn't / aren't playing the drums.

3
You aren't / isn't listening.

4
We isn't / aren't running.

5
I aren't / 'm not singing.

6
She isn't / aren't watching TV.

G **Write.**

> look   play   ride   sit   swim   ~~wear~~

1   She _isn't wearing_ a scarf.
    She _'s wearing_ a hat.

2   He _____ volleyball.
    He _____ basketball.

3   They _____ bikes.
    They _____ scooters.

4   He _____ in the sea.
    He _____ in a pool.

5   I _____ at a photo.
    I _____ at you!

6   We _____ in the classroom.
    We _____ in a rollercoaster.

H **Write.**

1   I'm reading a book. (not write)
    I'm not writing.

2   Sam is watching TV. (not sleep)
    _____

3   Pip and Susie are playing tennis. (not play football)
    _____

4   We are singing a song. (not listen to music)
    _____

5   The cat is eating its food. (not run)
    _____

Unit 10

Present Continuous – question and short answer

To ask if a person is doing an action now, we put **Am**, **Are**, **Is** at the beginning of the question. We can answer with **Yes** or **No**, the person and **am**, **are** or **is**.

Am I cook**ing**?	Yes, I **am**. / No, **I'm not**.
Are you cook**ing**?	Yes, you **are**. / No, you **aren't**.
Is he cook**ing**?	Yes, he **is**. / No, he **isn't**.
Is she cook**ing**?	Yes, she **is**. / No, she **isn't**.
Is it cook**ing**?	Yes, it **is**. / No, it **isn't**.
Are we cook**ing**?	Yes, we **are**. / No, we **aren't**.
Are you cook**ing**?	Yes, you **are**. / No, you **aren't**.
Are they cook**ing**?	Yes, they **are**. / No, they **aren't**.

I Write.

1
Is she playing tennis?
Yes, she is.

2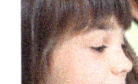
Are they drawing?
_____

3
Is he reading a book?
_____

4
Am I playing football?
_____

J Write and answer with a tick (✓) or cross (✗).

1. ? / your teacher / is / dancing
   <u>Is your teacher dancing?</u> ✗

2. ? / your friends / playing / are
   _____ ☐

3. ? / you / are / writing
   _____ ☐

4. ? / thinking / are / you
   _____ ☐

5. ? / the pupils / sitting / are
   _____ ☐

6. ? / a bird / is / singing
   _____ ☐

7. ? / your friend / reading / is
   _____ ☐

8. ? / having fun / you / are
   _____ ☐

K Write.

1. <u>Is</u> he <u>eating</u>? (eat)
   <u>Yes, he is.</u>

2. ____ he _____? (kick the ball)
   _____

3. ____ she _____? (cook)
   _____

4. ____ they _____? (have fun)
   _____

5. ____ she _____? (climb)
   _____

Unit 10

What ... doing?

We use **What** at the beginning of a question to ask what a person is doing now, or when we can see what a person is doing, but we want to ask more about the action.

What are you doing?   I'm climbing.
What are they doing?   They're singing.

L **Match.**

1 What are you doing?   a They're eating cake.
2 What am I doing?   b I'm riding a bike.
3 What is she doing?   c We're having fun.
4 What are they doing?   d She's climbing a mountain.
5 What are we doing?   e You're playing basketball.

Speaking

Say.
- climb
- ~~dance~~
- eat
- play basketball
- play tennis
- ride a bike
- sing
- sleep
- swim
- watch TV

What am I doing?
Are you swimming?
No, I'm not.
Are you dancing?
Yes, I am!

Imperative, Let's

Imperative – affirmative

To give instructions or orders, we only use the verb for the action. It doesn't matter how many people we are talking to.

Stand up!

A Match.

Listen!

Sit down!

Stand up!

Be quiet!

Open your books!

Stop!

1
2
3

4
5
6

B Circle.

1 **Run!** / Walk! That's the bus!
2 I can dance. Listen! / Watch!
3 Look! / Listen! The fireworks are great!
4 Go / Do your homework!
5 Sing / Talk the happy birthday song!

50

Unit 11

Imperative – negative

To tell a person not to do an action, we put **Don't** at the beginning of the sentence and before the verb.

Don't jump on the bed!

C **Write.**

Don't go on the ride!   ~~Don't pick the flowers!~~   Don't play with fireworks!
Don't sit down!   Don't swim here!   Don't watch TV!

1 Don't pick the flowers!

4 _____

2 _____

5 _____

3 _____

6 _____

D Write.

eat
make
play
ride
sit
~~watch~~

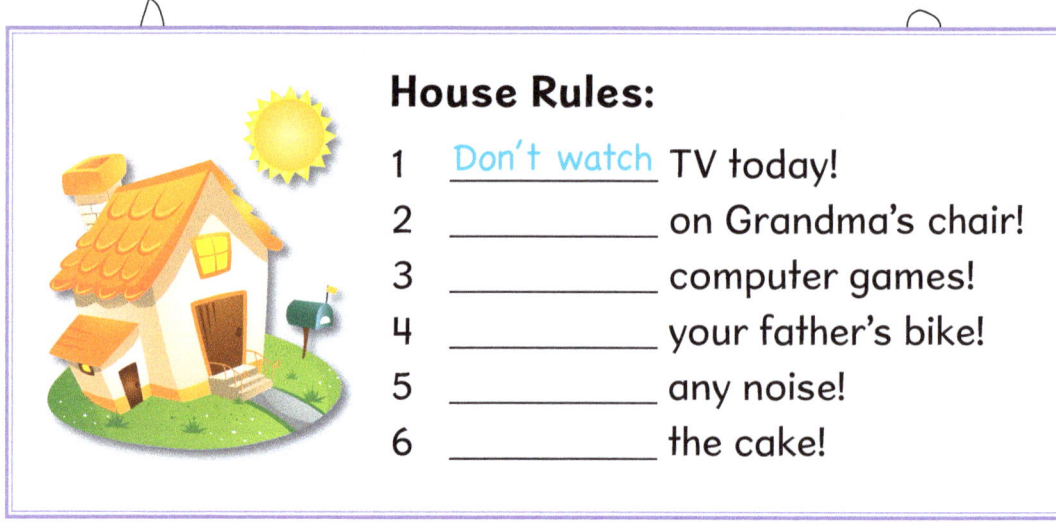

House Rules:
1 <u>Don't watch</u> TV today!
2 _____ on Grandma's chair!
3 _____ computer games!
4 _____ your father's bike!
5 _____ any noise!
6 _____ the cake!

E Match.

1 Look!   a It's cold outside.
2 Don't walk!   b I'm talking to you.
3 Don't eat those! c That cat is beautiful.
4 Listen to me!   d The light is red.
5 Wear your hat! e They aren't nice.

F Write.

1 Talk to the teacher. ____<u>Don't talk</u>____ to your friends.
2 Don't run in the classroom. _____ in the playground.
3 Look at the board. _____ at your book.
4 Write with a pencil. _____ with a pen.
5 _____ happy. Don't be sad.
6 Don't eat in the classroom. _____ in the dining room.

Unit 11

Let's

To suggest an action to other people, we use **Let's** at the beginning of the sentence and before the verb.

Let's run!

G Match.

1 It's Chinese New Year.
2 I'm hungry.
3 It's Mum's birthday today.
4 That's my favourite computer game.
5 This is a nice song.
6 The river is clean.

a Let's have a sandwich!
b Let's watch the fireworks!
c Let's buy a present!
d Let's swim!
e Let's sing!
f Let's play!

Speaking

Let's draw!

Say.

Plurals -es, -ies and Irregular Plurals

"Two families, eight babies!"

Plurals -es, -ies

When we talk about more than one person, animal or thing, we usually put **-s** at the end of the word.

one goat → two goat**s**

But when words end in **-s**, then we put **-es** at the end of the word.

one bus → two bus**es**

The same happens when words end in **-ss**, **-ch**, **-sh**, **-x**, **-o**.

one glass → five glass**es**
one beach → six beach**es**
one dish → four dish**es**
one fox → two fox**es**
one potato → seven potato**es**

When words end in a consonant + **-y**, then we drop the **-y** and we add **-ies** at the end of the word.

one baby → three bab**ies**
one family → two famil**ies**

But when words end in a vowel + **-y**, we add only **-s**.

one toy → ten toy**s**
one boy → three boy**s**

54

Unit 12

A Write.

1 _____cars_____

4 _____

2 _____

5 _____

3 _____

6 _____

B Circle.

1 Let's go to the (beach) / beaches.
2 Dad's got two red shirt / shirts.
3 This is my family / families.
4 There is a dish / dishes on the table.
5 Paul's got three new toy / toys.
6 He's eating tomato / tomatoes.

C Write.

1 one dress   →   two _____dresses_____
2 one family   →   four _____
3 one monkey   →   three _____
4 one boy   →   six _____
5 one box   →   five _____
6 one dish   →   seven _____

There isn't one mouse. There are lots of mice!

Plurals – irregular

There are some words which have a different - an irregular - form in the plural.

child → child**ren**
foot → f**ee**t
man → m**e**n
mouse → m**ice**
tooth → t**ee**th
woman → wom**e**n

D **Write.**

1  child →  children

2 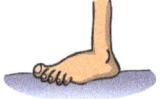 _____ → 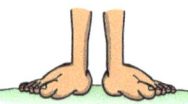 _____

3  _____ →  _____

4 _____ →  _____

5  _____ → _____ _____

6  _____ →  _____

Unit 12

E Write.

~~baby~~ ~~bike~~ ~~bus~~ cherry ~~child~~ city dish face family fly
foot fox glass man mouse ostrich party river shirt
shop tomato tooth toy woman

-s	-es	-ies	!
bikes	buses	babies	children

Speaking

C1? Babies!

Say.

Review 3 (Units 9-12)

A Write **can** or **can't**.

1 He __can__ jump. 2 She _____ swim. 3 They _____ sing.

4 They _____ run. 5 It _____ read. 6 We _____ dance.

B Look and write.

	Lyn	Alex	Maya	Philip
dance	✔			
play volleyball	✔		✔	
swim	✔	✔		✔
sing	✔			
play the piano			✔	✔

1 __Can__ Alex sing?   No, he can't.
2 _____ Lyn and Maya play volleyball?   _____
3 _____ Philip swim?   _____
4 _____ Lyn dance?   _____
5 _____ Lyn and Alex play the piano?   _____

C Write and answer about yourself.

1 __Are__ you sleeping?   No, I'm not.
2 _____ your mum working?   _____
3 _____ your friends playing?   _____
4 _____ you writing?   _____
5 _____ your teacher standing? _____

Review 3

D Write.

climb   eat   ~~have~~   play   ride   sleep

1
What are they doing?
They __'re having__ fun.

2
What _____ it doing?
It _____ in its bed.

3
_____ is she doing?
She _____ a rollercoaster.

4
What is he _____?
He _____ a mountain.

5
What am I _____?
You _____ baseball.

6
What _____ you doing?
We _____ birthday cake.

E Match.

1 Don't eat   a at me!
2 Let's draw   b a picture!
3 Look   c to sleep!
4 Clean   d your shoes!
5 Don't go   e my dinner!

F Write.

baby   bus   ~~dress~~   mouse   pupil   tooth

1 Mary has got five red ___dresses___ .
2 There are twenty _____ in my class.
3 I take two _____ to go to school.
4 _____ drink milk.
5 Minnie and Mickey are _____ .
6 Our _____ are white.

Some and Any

Some and any

To talk about an amount of people, animals or things we use **some** and **any**. We use **some** in affirmative sentences and we use **any** in negative sentences and in questions.

I've got **some** pencils.
She hasn't got **any** pencils.
Have they got **any** pencils?

The same happens when we use there is / there are.

There are **some** notebooks in the kitchen.

There aren't **any** computers in the classroom.

Are there **any** books on the desk?

A Write **some** or **any**.

1 There are ____some____ notebooks on the desk.

2 Lucy hasn't got _____ toys in her bag.

3 The boys haven't got _____ green pens, but they have got _____ blue pens.

4 I've got _____ pencils, but I haven't got _____ rubbers.

5 Grandma's got _____ bananas and _____ cherries for us.

6 There aren't _____ children in the park.

Unit 13

B Match.

1 Has a dog got — d any fingers?
2 There is — a some spots.
3 Leo the leopard has got — b any teeth?
4 Look! There are — c some sugar on the table.
5 Have snakes got — e any tigers in the sea.
6 There aren't — f some fireworks in the sky.

C Write have got, haven't got, has got or hasn't got with some or any.

1
She ___hasn't got any___ eggs.

4
I _____ flippers.

2
She _____ apples.

5
The baby _____ milk.

3
We _____ books.

6
The dog _____ water.

61

Prepositions of Place, Where is ...?/ Where are ...?

"Ty! You're standing on my tail."

Prepositions of place

We use **prepositions of place** to say where a person, animal or thing is.

on
The cat is **on** the chair.

in
The book is **in** the bag.

under
The socks are **under** the chair.

behind
The woman is **behind** the man.

in front of
The boys are **in front of** the desk.

next to
The toy is **next to** the bike.

A Write.

behind   in   ~~in front of~~   next to   on   under

1. ___in front of___

2. _____

3. _____

4. _____

5. _____

6. _____

Unit 14

B **Read and draw.**

1   The house is behind the girl.

2   The skateboard is next to the boy.

3   The ball is under the table.

4   The car is in front of the cinema.

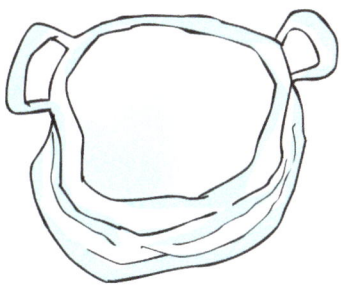

5   The flippers and the mask are in the bag.

6   There's a spider on Mum's head!

Say.

- ~~apples/bananas~~
- basket/door
- carrots/potatoes
- cat/chair
- man/chair
- pencil/notebook
- potatoes/basket
- tomatoes/carrots

There are some apples next to the bananas.

Where is ...?/Where are ...?

When we ask about the place a person, animal or thing is, we use **Where is ...?** We use **Where are ...?** for many people, animals or things.

Where is the basket?
Where are the sweets?

Note
There is a short form: **Where is** → **Where's**

C Write.

1 Where is Mary's notebook?
   Where's Mary's notebook?

2 Where is the DVD?
   _____

3 Where is Mike?
   _____

4 Where is the milk?
   _____

5 Where is the basket?
   _____

6 Where is the cheese?
   _____

D Circle.

1 Where (is) / are the boat?
2 Where is / are the drums?
3 Where is / are your boots?
4 Where is / are Jack's T-shirt?
5 Where is / are the mice?
6 Where is / are my bike?

Unit 14

E **Write Where is or Where are and match.**

1. _Where are_ the apples? — a She's in the kitchen.
2. _____ the cheese? — b They're in the box.
3. _____ Tamsin? — c It's under the butter.
4. _____ the milk? — d They're behind the door.
5. _____ the sweets? — e It's on the table.
6. _____ my shoes? — f They're next to the cake.

Speaking

Where's the ball?

It's behind the CDs.

Say.
- ball/CDs
- books/computer
- CDs/box
- chair/desk
- computer/desk
- cat/desk
- lion/bed
- pens/book
- skateboard/bed
- teddy bears/bed

Present Simple

Present Simple – affirmative (1)

We use the **Present Simple** to say what happens, or that a person does an action *always, often, every day* or *usually*. We use the person (**I**, **you**, **we**, etc) and the verb only in affirmative sentences. The verb changes with **he** / **she** / **it**. Then we must add **-s** at the end of the verb.

I swim
you swim
he swim**s**
she swim**s**
it swim**s**
we swim
you swim
they swim

I **ride** my bike on Friday.
He cook**s** on Sunday.

A   Circle.

1   On Monday, Mum play / (plays) tennis.
2   On Tuesday, you cook / cooks dinner.
3   On Wednesday, James and Matt walk / walks to school.
4   On Thursday, we sing / sings songs at school.
5   On Friday, Timothy eat / eats pizza.
6   On Saturday, I get / gets up at 9 o'clock.

Unit 15

B Write.

1 Sam and Milly _____eat_____ (eat) an apple every day.
2 I _____ (play) volleyball on Monday.
3 Jason _____ (sit) at the front of the class.
4 My mum _____ (cook) yummy cakes.
5 Maggie's sister _____ (listen) to great music!
6 You _____ (run) very fast!
7 My brother _____ (read) books at the weekends.
8 Rick's rabbit _____ (like) carrots.

C Write and match.

| ~~drive~~   play   ride   sit   wear   win |

1 Dad ___drives___ big cars.   a

2 I _____ the guitar on Sunday.   b

3 The girls _____ pink socks every day.   c

4 Tom _____ next to Elliot at school.   d

5 Our teacher _____ a bike to school.   e

6 Max _____ the cup every year.   f

Present Simple – affirmative (2)

When the verb ends in **-sh**, **-ch**, **-o** and we have **he** / **she** / **it**, we add **-es** at the end of the verb.

Mike watch**es** TV on Saturday.

When the verb ends in a consonant **+ -y** and we have **he** / **she** / **it**, we drop the **-y** and we add **-ies** at the end of the verb.

Shelly stud**ies** English on Mondays and Wednesdays.

D Write.

1 My sister stud_ies_ a lot.
2 My dog like____ chocolate.
3 Our cat watch____ TV.
4 My brother go____ to a big school.
5 An aeroplane fl____ fast.
6 She listen____ to music in her bedroom.

E Write.

1 We go to school. He _goes to school_ .
2 I try hard. It _____ .
3 We wash the glasses. He _____ .
4 I stand next to the desk. She _____ .
5 You ride a bike. He _____ .

Unit 15

F Write.

brush   ~~get up~~   go   play   study   watch

1

Flo ___gets up___ at 7 o'clock.

4

She _____ hard at school.

2

Her mum _____ her hair.

5

She _____ in the park.

3

Flo _____ to school on the bus.

6

At night, she _____ TV.

Speaking

Sam gets up at 7 o'clock.

Say.

- do his homework
- have breakfast
- ~~get up at 7 o'clock~~
- play with his friends
- go to bed at 9 o'clock
- study hard at school

1    2    3

4    5    6

Present Simple – negative

To say that an action doesn't happen or that a person doesn't do an action *always*, *often*, *every day* or *usually*, we use the **Present Simple** with **do not** (**don't**) or **does not** (**doesn't**) before the verb.

We use **does not** with **he / she / it**, and with **I / you / we / you / they** we use **don't**. When we have **does not** (**doesn't**), we don't add **-s**, **-es**, or **-ies** at the end of the verb.

When we speak, we usually use the short form.

I **do not** swim   I **don't** swim
you **do not** swim   you **don't** swim
he **does not** swim   he **doesn't** swim
she **does not** swim   she **doesn't** swim
it **does not** swim   it **doesn't** swim
we **do not** swim   we **don't** swim
you **do not** swim   you **don't** swim
they **do not** swim   they **don't** swim

She **doesn't eat** breakfast.)
They **don't play** tennis on Saturdays.

G **Circle.**

1. I (**don't**) / doesn't go to school on Sunday.
2. He don't / doesn't ride a bike.
3. We don't / doesn't go to the theatre.
4. It don't / doesn't eat bread.
5. Mum and Dad don't / doesn't watch TV.
6. She don't / doesn't sing very well!

Unit 15

H Write **don't** or **doesn't**.

Mr and Mrs No (1) ___don't___ like anything! Mr No (2) _____ eat vegetables. Mrs No (3) _____ eat meat. Martha and Rick (4) _____ play games. He (5) _____ like balls and she (6) _____ wear trainers! The Nos (7) _____ have any friends. They (8) _____ like people!

I Write.

climb   eat   go   play   ride   ~~wear~~

1  Mum ___wears___ trousers. She ___doesn't wear___ dresses.

2  Dad _____ crisps. He _____ popcorn.

3  They _____ basketball. They _____ tennis.

4  He _____ a bike. He _____ a scooter.

5  I _____ mountains. I _____ trees.

6  We _____ to the theatre. We _____ to the cinema.

Present Simple – question and short answer

To form a question with the **Present Simple**, we put **Do** or **Does** at the beginning of the question. When we use **does**, we don't add **-s**, **-es** or **-ies** at the end of the verb. We can give short answers with **Yes** or **No**, the person and **do** / **does** or **don't** / **doesn't**.

Do I swim?	Yes, I **do**. / No, I **don't**.
Do you swim?	Yes, you **do**. / No, you **don't**.
Does he swim?	Yes, he **does**. / No, he **doesn't**.
Does she swim?	Yes, she **does**. / No, she **doesn't**.
Does it swim?	Yes, it **does**. / No, it **doesn't**.
Do we swim?	Yes, we **do**. / No, we **don't**.
Do you swim?	Yes, you **do**. / No, you **don't**.
Do they swim?	Yes, they **do**. / No, they **don't**.

Do you **like** oranges?
Yes, I **do**. / No, I **don't**.

Does Peter **get up** at 7 o'clock?
Yes, he **does**. / No, he **doesn't**.

J Match.

1 Does Dean like cameras?   a Yes, you do.
2 Does Laura go to school?   b No, I don't.
3 Do you eat crisps?   c Yes, he does.
4 Does your dog live in a box?   d No, it doesn't.
5 Do cats drink milk?   e Yes, they do.
6 Do we run at school?   f No, she doesn't.

Unit 15

K Write.

1  ____Do____ they go to school?   Yes, they do.

2  _____ he like the food?   _____

3 ![dolphin] _____ it swim in the sea?   _____

4  _____ they work in a garden?   _____

Speaking

Do you watch TV?   Yes, I do.

Write and say.

- eat
- listen to
- play
- ride
- ~~watch~~

Do you ...	You	Your friend
📺	✔	✔
🎾		
🚲		
🎧		
🍳		

16 Prepositions of time, What ... + prepositions of time, Question words

Prepositions of time

We use **prepositions of time** to say when something happens.

in

in the morning   in the evening
in the afternoon   in spring

I have a piano lesson **in** the evening.

on

on Monday   on Friday
on Wednesday   on Saturday

Mike plays football **on** Sunday.

at

at 7 o'clock   at night
at 3 o'clock   at the weekend

We cook **at** 5 o'clock every day.

A Write **at**, **in** or **on**.

1. Kyle drinks milk ___in___ the morning.
2. We get up _____ 7 o'clock.
3. It's cold _____ winter.
4. I go to school _____ Monday.
5. I play tennis _____ the weekend.

Unit 16

What ... + prepositions of time

To ask what a person does *every morning, every evening, every Saturday*, etc, we use the word **What** at the beginning of the question.

What do you do **on Saturday**?
What does Angela do **in the evening**?
What do they do **at the weekend**?

B Write.

1 _What does Sue do_ in the morning?
   Sue goes to the park.

2 _____ in the evening?
   Mark watches TV.

3 _____ at the weekend?
   I go to the cinema.

4 _____ on Sunday?
   They do their homework.

5 _____ at 8 o'clock?
   Lisa gets up.

6 _____ every day?
   We brush our teeth.

Speaking

Write and say.

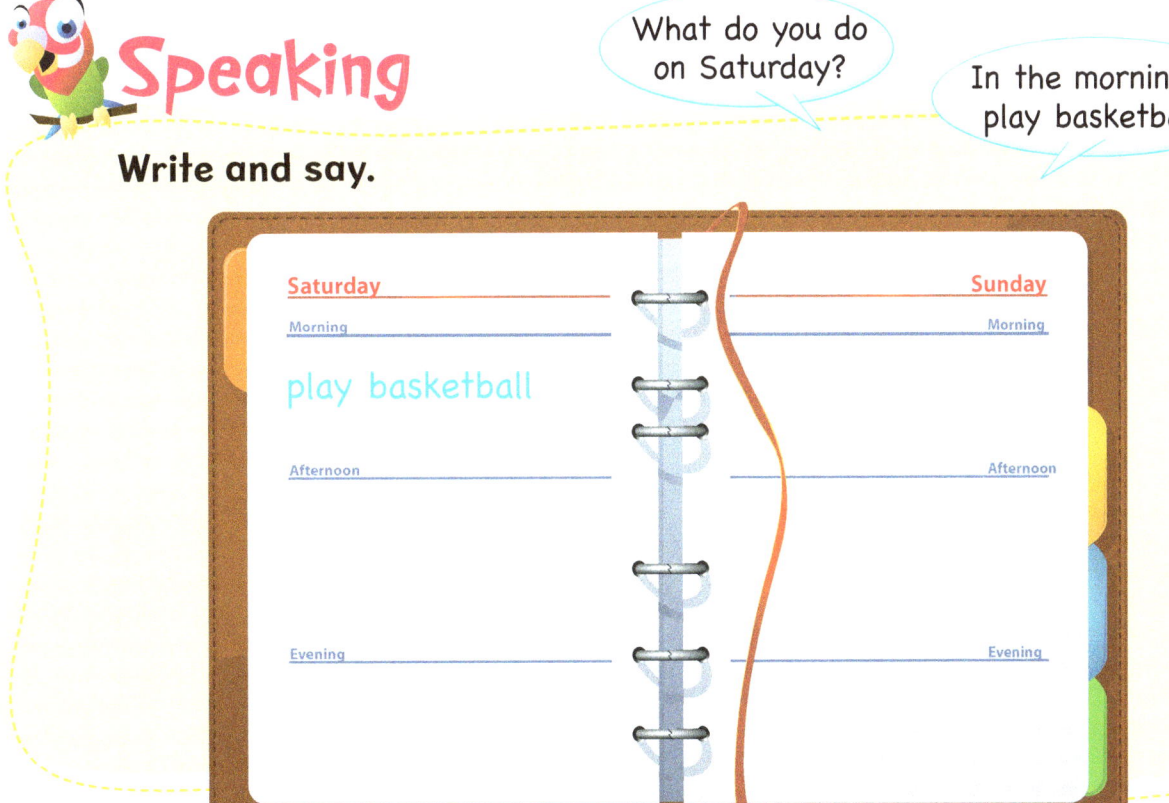

Question words

We use question words when we want more information than **yes** or **no** in the answer.

We use **What** to ask about things and actions.

What is this?
It's my bag.

What is Jessica doing?
She is swimming.

We use **When** to ask about time.

When is your English lesson?
On Monday.

We use **Where** to ask about a place.

Where is my book?
In your bedroom.

Where are your friends?
At the park.

We use **Who** to ask about people.

Who is he?
He is my brother, Tom.

C   Match.

1   Where are your shoes?
2   Where is my schoolbag?
3   What is that?
4   Who is Tom?
5   What are you doing?
6   When is the maths lesson?

a   It's a cave.
b   We're playing a game.
c   It's on Monday.
d   It's under the bed.
e   He's my brother.
f   They're in the kitchen.

Unit 16

D **Circle.**

1. A: (Who) / When is she?
   B: She's my friend.

2. A: What / Where are they?
   B: They're dragonflies.

3. A: Where / Who is the goat?
   B: It's in the garden.

4. A: What / Who is that?
   B: That's the new teacher.

5. A: When / What are the holidays?
   B: They're in summer.

6. A: Where / What is in your bag?
   B: It's a toy cat.

7. A: What / Where is she doing?
   B: She's sleeping.

8. A: Who / Where are the books?
   B: They're on the desk.

What's your name?

My name is Michalis.

Write and say.

	You	Your friend
1 What's your name?	Alex	Michalis
2 Who is your best friend?		
3 What's your favourite animal?		
4 Where is your school?		
5 Where do you go on holiday?		
6 When is your birthday?		

Review 4 (Units 13–16)

A Look and write **have got** or **haven't got** with **some** and **any**.

What's in my bag? I (1) __have got some__ notebooks. I (2) _____ books. I (3) _____ pens but I (4) _____ pencils. I (5) _____ sweets and I (6) _____ apples. Oh no! I (7) _____ socks too! Are there any socks in your bag?

B Write.

| behind | in | ~~in front of~~ |
| next to | on | under |

1 __Where is__ Sally?
   She's __in front of__ the door.
2 _____ Tom?
   He's _____ the door.
3 _____ the chair?
   It's _____ the door.
4 _____ Tom's shoes?
   They're _____ the chair.
5 _____ Tom's bag?
   It's _____ the chair.
6 _____ Tom's hat?
   It's _____ the bag.
7 _____ Tom's socks?
   They're _____ the bag.

C Write.

1 Kim / play / football (✔)   __Kim plays football.__
2 Tom / play / tennis (✘)   _____
3 He / fly / a plane (✔)   _____
4 Mum / watch / TV (✔)   _____
5 Karl / swim / in the river (✘) _____
6 I / climb / mountains (✘)   _____

Review 4

D Circle and write about you.

1 Do / (Does) your mum make cakes?   Yes, she does.
2 Do / Does you live in a city?   _____
3 Do / Does you like bananas?   _____
4 Do / Does your friends play football?   _____
5 Do / Does your dad drive a car?   _____

E Write.

1 ? / do / they / what / do / in the evening
What do they do in the evening?
They watch TV in the evening.

2 ? / Nancy / does / practise / on Monday / what
_____
_____

3 ? / do / what / they / do / at the weekend
_____
_____

4 ? / study / Brian / what / does / on Tuesday
_____
_____

5 ? / what / drink / Frankie / does / in the morning
_____
_____

6 ? / at night / Valerie / what / do / does
_____
_____

F Write and match.

| what   what   when   where   ~~who~~ |

1 __Who__ is Shrek?   a It's in winter.
2 _____ is London?   b It's an animal.
3 _____ is a hippopotamus?   c TV.
4 _____ is New Year?   d It's in England.
5 _____ are you watching?   e He's a monster.

Wordlist

Unit 1

Page 4
1:1 fly
1:2 elephant
1:3 baby
1:4 panda
1:5 song
1:6 octopus
1:7 girl
1:8 quilt
1:9 egg
1:10 dog
1:11 car
1:12 insect
1:13 fox

Page 5
1:14 nice
1:15 blue
1:16 pencil
1:17 cat
1:18 brother
1:19 me
1:20 mum
1:21 dad
1:22 king
1:23 sister
1:24 spider
1:25 worm

Unit 2

Pages 6-7
2:1 leopard
2:2 meerkat
2:3 frog
2:4 green
2:5 robot
2:6 fantastic
2:7 cool
2:8 friend
2:9 pupil
2:10 name
2:11 England
2:12 Look!!
2:13 photo
2:14 too
2:15 grandma
2:16 happy
2:17 grandpa
2:18 all

Pages 8-9
2:19 toy
2:20 camera
2:21 funny
2:22 short
2:23 teddy bear
2:24 best
2:25 boy
2:26 cake
2:27 brown
2:28 ant
2:29 igloo
2:30 ball
2:31 tall
2:32 Africa
2:33 fun

Pages 10-11
2:34 giraffe
2:35 birthday cake
2:36 small
2:37 yummy
2:38 Are you OK?
2:39 hunter

Unit 3

Pages 12-13
3:1 one
3:2 banana
3:3 monkey
3:4 hat
3:5 candle
3:6 house
3:7 bird

Unit 4

Page 14
4:1 animal
4:2 flower
4:3 rabbit
4:4 lion
4:5 dolphin
4:6 whale
4:7 sandwich
4:8 computer game

Page 15
4:9 orange
4:10 hungry
4:11 big
4:12 nice
4:13 ostrich
4:14 tree

Pages 16-17
4:15 shark
4:16 penguin
4:17 skateboard
4:18 present

Wordlist

Unit 5

Pages 20-21
5:1 beach
5:2 rock
5:3 book
5:4 desk
5:5 helicopter
5:6 lizard
5:7 snake
5:8 sea
5:9 teacher
5:10 classroom
5:11 school
5:12 bear
5:13 class)
5:14 drawing
5:15 crisps
5:16 apple
5:17 bottle of lemonade
5:18 pink
5:19 three

Pages 22-23
5:20 any
5:21 pen
5:22 twenty
5:23 box
5:24 Australia
5:25 bag
5:26 unit
5:27 ten
5:28 bedroom
5:29 fifteen
5:30 yo-yo
5:31 computer
5:32 six
5:33 board
5:34 notebook
5:35 five
5:36 yellow
5:37 umbrella

Page 24
5:38 Look out!
5:39 bus

Page 25
5:40 eleven

Unit 6

Pages 26-27
6:1 wave
6:2 sun
6:3 sky
6:4 moon
6:5 outside
6:6 garden
6:7 purple
6:8 aeroplane
6:9 chair
6:10 two
6:11 black
6:12 red
6:13 orange
6:14 grey

Unit 7

Pages 28-29
7:1 eight
7:2 leg
7:3 long
7:4 tongue
7:5 tail
7:6 eye
7:7 toe
7:8 kangaroo
7:9 ear
7:10 nose
7:11 wet
7:12 hair
7:13 sad
7:14 tarantula
7:15 teeth

Pages 30-31
7:16 bicycle
7:17 thin
7:18 fat
7:19 pet
7:20 surfboard
7:21 picnic
7:22 beach umbrella
7:23 rubber
7:24 ruler

Pages 32-33
7:25 flippers
7:26 TV
7:27 arm)
7:28 fourteen
7:29 finger

Unit 8

Pages 34-35
8:1 sock
8:2 mobile phone
8:3 shoe
8:4 shirt
8:5 dress
8:6 mask
8:7 sweets
8:8 milk
8:9 cold
8:10 jeans
8:11 new
8:12 old

Wordlist

Unit 9

Page 38
9:1 can
9:2 dance
9:3 samba
9:4 sing
9:5 run
9:6 parrot
9:7 speak
9:8 koala
9:9 jump
9:10 dancer
9:11 read
9:12 swim

Page 39
9:13 see
9:14 play
9:15 sit down
9:16 draw
9:17 walk

Pages 40-41
9:18 play the drums
9:19 play the guitar
9:20 play tennis
9:21 play volleyball
9:22 piano
9:23 fly
9:24 climb
9:25 eat

Unit 10

Pages 42-44
10:1 ride a bike
10:2 cook
10:3 write
10:4 sit
10:5 watch
10:6 game
10:7 sleep
10:8 listen
10:9 bed
10:10 music
10:11 circus school
10:12 have fun
10:13 zebra
10:14 head
10:15 wear

Pages 45-46
10:16 scarf
10:17 basketball
10:18 scooter
10:19 pool
10:20 rollercoaster
10:21 play football
10:22 food

Pages 47-48
10:23 wrong
10:24 T-shirt
10:25 think
10:26 kick

Page 49
10:27 do
10:28 mountain

Unit 11

Page 50
11:1 Stand up!
11:2 Be quiet!
11:3 Open your books!
11:4 Stop!
11:5 fireworks
11:6 great
11:7 go
11:8 do homework
11:9 happy birthday song

Pages 51-52
11:10 Don't move!
11:11 Don't go on the ride!
11:12 Don't pick the flowers!
11:13 here
11:14 make
11:15 rules
11:16 today
11:17 noise
11:18 It's cold outside.
11:19 I'm talking to you.
11:20 beautiful
11:21 light
11:22 playground
11:23 dining room

Page 53
11:24 tired
11:25 Let's go home.
11:26 Chinese
11:27 New Year
11:28 birthday
11:29 favourite
11:30 river
11:31 clean
11:32 Let's have a sandwich!
11:33 buy

Unit 12

Pages 54-55
12:1 family
12:2 goat

Wordlist

12:3	glass		15:8	very
12:4	dish		15:9	fast
12:5	a potato		15:10	at the weekend
12:6	a table		15:11	night
12:7	a tomato		15:12	drive
			15:13	win
			15:14	Sunday
			15:15	a cup
			15:16	every year

Pages 56-57
- 12:8 a mouse
- 12:9 lots of
- 12:10 a child
- 12:11 a foot
- 12:12 a man
- 12:13 a tooth
- 12:14 a woman
- 12:15 a cherry
- 12:16 a city
- 12:17 a face
- 12:18 a party
- 12:19 a shop

Pages 68-69
- 15:17 wash
- 15:18 tidy
- 15:19 Saturday
- 15:20 study
- 15:21 Wednesday
- 15:22 a lot
- 15:23 try hard
- 15:24 brush
- 15:25 get up
- 15:26 have breakfast
- 15:27 study hard

Unit 13

Pages 60-61
- 13:1 some
- 13:2 chocolate
- 13:3 a kitchen
- 13:4 a park
- 13:5 a spot
- 13:6 sugar
- 13:7 a tiger
- 13:8 water

Pages 70-71
- 15:28 a theatre
- 15:29 bread
- 15:30 well
- 15:31 like
- 15:32 anything
- 15:33 a vegetable
- 15:34 meat
- 15:35 trainers
- 15:36 people
- 15:37 trousers
- 15:38 popcorn

Unit 14

Pages 62-63
- 14:1 stand
- 14:2 a cinema
- 14:3 a basket
- 14:4 carrots
- 14:5 a door

Unit 16

Page 74
- 16:1 in the morning
- 16:2 afternoon
- 16:3 evening
- 16:4 spring
- 16:5 a lesson
- 16:6 Friday
- 16:7 winter

Pages 64-65
- 14:6 clothes
- 14:7 a boat
- 14:8 a boot
- 14:9 cheese
- 14:10 butter

Pages 76-77
- 16:8 a schoolbag
- 16:9 maths
- 16:10 a cave
- 16:11 a dragonfly
- 16:12 holidays

Unit 15

Pages 66-67
- 15:1 clean
- 15:2 dinner
- 15:3 a pizza
- 15:4 9 o'clock
- 15:5 every day
- 15:6 Monday
- 15:7 at the front

Test 1 (Units 1-4)

A Circle.

1 **a** / an ball
2 a / an yo-yo
3 a / an party
4 a / an ostrich
5 a / an penguin

6 a / an octopus
7 a / an igloo
8 a / an hat
9 a / an egg
10 a / an ant

.... / 9 marks

B Match.

1 Mum and Dad
2 my sister
3 my brother
4 my cat
5 me and my friends
6 you and your friends
7 me

a it
b she
c we
d they
e you
f he
g I

.... / 6 marks

C Write This, That, These or Those.

1 ____This____ is a skateboard.

5 _____ is a beach.

2 _____ is a toy.

6 _____ are lizards.

3 _____ are presents.

7 _____ are elephants.

4 _____ are teddy bears.

8 _____ is my sister.

.... / 7 marks

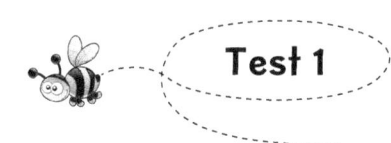

Test 1

D Count and write.

1
  one dog   four dogs

2
  one monkey   _____

3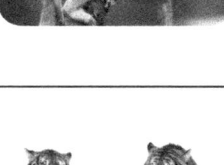
  one tiger   _____

4
  one bird   _____

5
  one insect   _____

6
  one meerkat   _____

/ 5 marks

E Write am, is or are.

1 Ty __is__ a panda.
2 I ____ nine years old.
3 ____ you my friend?
4 We ____ from Africa.
5 My dog ____ black and white.
6 Leo and Mia ____ funny!
7 My sister ____ cool.

/ 6 marks

F Write am, aren't, is or isn't.

1  This elephant __isn't__ small. It __'s__ big.

2  I _____ seven. I ____ nine.

3  They _____ Mum and Dad. They ____ Grandma and Grandpa.

4  We _____ penguins. We ____ dolphins.

5  Africa _____ small. It ____ big.

6  He _____ happy. He ____ sad.

/ 5 marks

Test 1

G Write and match.

1 __Is__   Mia a lion? a No, she isn't.
2 _____ you a teacher? b Yes, it is.
3 _____ Ty and Leo friends? c Yes, they are.
4 _____ you and your friends happy? d No, they aren't.
5 _____ a whale big? e No, I'm not.
6 _____ giraffes short? f Yes, we are.

.... / 5 marks

H Write What's this? What's that? What are these? or What are those?

1 __What's that?__ It's a tree.

5 _____ It's a giraffe.

2 _____ They're boys.

6 _____ It's a car.

3 _____ It's a snake.

7 _____ They're houses.

4 _____ They're ants.

8 _____ They're bananas.

.... / 7 marks

.... / 50 marks

Test 2 (Units 5-8)

A Circle.

In my classroom...
1 ... there **are** / is desks.
2 ... there **is** / **are** a teacher.
3 ... there **are** / **is** books.
4 ... there **isn't** / **aren't** a TV.
5 ... there **isn't** / **aren't** three pupils.
6 ... there **is** / **are** a computer.
7 ... there **aren't** / **isn't** any lions.
8 ... there **isn't** / **aren't** a tree.

_____ / 7 marks

B Write.

1 __How many__ notebooks __are there__ ? There are five notebooks.
2 _____ teachers _____ ? _____
3 _____ desks _____ ? _____
4 _____ pupils _____ ? _____
5 _____ books _____ ? _____

_____ / 4 marks

C Write.

1 Bob has got green eyes. __Bob's__ eyes are green.
2 Angela has got a bike. _____ bike is yellow.
3 Lucy has got a dog. _____ dog is brown.
4 Maria has got a teddy bear. _____ teddy bear is big.
5 Mike has got presents. _____ presents are great.
6 Mum has got a car. _____ car is red.

_____ / 5 marks

Test 2

D Write.

1. Is there a lion?
   Yes, there is.

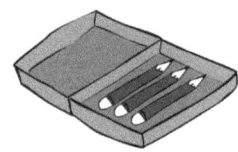

2. Are there any pens?
   _____

3. Are there thirteen apples?
   _____

4. Is there a skateboard?
   _____

5. Are there beaches in Australia?
   _____

6. Is there a helicopter in the sky? _____

_____ / 5 marks

E Write a, an or the.

What's in (1) __the__ box? There's (2) _____ nose, there's (3) _____ hat and there are trousers. (4) _____ hat is funny. It has got a flower on it. (5) _____ trousers have got stripes. There's (6) _____ big shoe and (7) _____ small shoe. Look at (8) _____ flippers! Are they for (9) _____ sea?

_____ / 8 marks

Test 2

F Write have got, has got, haven't got or hasn't got.

1 Leo __has got__ spots.
2 A rabbit _____ small ears.
3 My teacher _____ a notebook.
4 Giraffes _____ three legs.
5 Pupils _____ pencils.
6 A car _____ legs.
7 Elephants _____ long noses.
8 Frogs _____ hair.

_____ / 7 marks

G Write.

1 __Have__ the children __got__ balloons? __Yes, they have.__
2 _____ they _____ toys?
   _____
3 _____ the girl _____ a bike?
   _____
4 _____ they _____ a cat?
   _____
5 _____ the boy _____ black hair?
   _____
6 _____ they _____ a skateboard?
   _____

_____ / 5 marks

H Circle.

1 Mia and Ty are friends. (Their) / His favourite food is sweets.
2 Leo is a leopard. His / Her spots are black.
3 My mum is beautiful. Her / His hair is red.
4 Me and Trek are friends. Our / Their computer games are pink.
5 That's a nice dog. His / Its nose is white.
6 I'm a monster. Our / My eyes are yellow.
7 You are a cat. Its / Your tail is short.
8 Grandma and Grandpa are happy. Their / Your car is new.
9 You are pupils. Your / Their notebooks are on the desk.
10 My friends are happy. Your / Their mum and dad are playing with them.

_____ / 9 marks

_____ / 50 marks

Test 3 (Units 9-12)

A Circle.

1 Penguins (can) / can't swim.
2 Pianos can / can't jump.
3 Snakes can / can't ride a bike.
4 Birds can / can't fly.
5 Whales can / can't run.
6 Dolphins can / can't read.
7 Parrots can't / can swim.
8 Pupils can / can't read.
9 Ants can / can't sing.
10 Cats can / can't sleep.

_____ / 9 marks

B Write.

cook   dance   go   play   ride   run

1 __Can__ he __cook__?
   No, he can't.

2 _____ he _____ a bike?
   _____

3 _____ they _____?
   _____

4 _____ she _____ tennis?
   _____

5 _____ he _____?
   _____

6 _____ it _____ fast?
   _____

_____ / 5 marks

Test 3

C Circle.

1 Debbie (is) / are eating.
2 Robin isn't / aren't playing tennis.
3 I am / is riding my bike.
4 Mum and Dad am not / aren't sleeping.
5 Leo aren't / isn't dancing.
6 We are / is listening to music.
7 That dog is / am jumping.
8 I 'm not / aren't eating a sandwich.

.... / 7 marks

D Write.

1 __Are__ you watching TV?   No, __I'm not__ .
2 _____ Ty and Mia having fun?   Yes, _____ .
3 _____ Trek playing basketball?   No, _____ .
4 _____ you listening to the teacher?   Yes, _____ .
5 _____ Leo climbing a mountain?   Yes, _____ .
6 _____ you and your friends reading?   Yes, _____ .

.... / 5 marks

E Circle.

SCHOOL RULES
1 (Listen) / Don't listen to the teacher.
2 Eat / Don't eat in the classroom.
3 Play / Don't play games in the playground.
4 Sit / Don't sit on the chairs.
5 Read / Don't read the lesson.
6 Write / Don't write on the desks.
7 Open / Don't open your books.

.... / 6 marks

F Write.

climb   eat   have   play   read   swim   ~~watch~~

1 It's New Year. __Let's watch__ the fireworks!
2 I'm hungry. _____ a sandwich!
3 This is a great book. _____ it!
4 The sea is nice. _____ !
5 It's my birthday. _____ fun!
6 That's a big tree. _____ it!
7 I've got a new computer game. _____ !

.... / 6 marks

Test 3

G Write.

1. dress → _dresses_
2. family → _____
3. child → _____
4. tooth → _____
5. woman → _____
6. mouse → _____
7. foot → _____
8. potato → _____

_____ / 7 marks

H Look and write.

cook   kick   listen   play   ~~ride~~   sing

1. What are they doing?
   They're riding their bikes.

2. What's she doing?
   _____ the ball.

3. What are they doing?
   _____ biscuits.

4. What's he doing?
   _____ baseball.

5. What's she doing?
   _____ a song.

6. What are they doing?
   _____ to the teacher.

_____ / 5 marks

_____ / 50 marks

Test 4 (Units 13-16)

A Circle.

1. My dog hasn't got some / (any) spots.
2. Have you got some / any sugar?
3. I have got some / any red socks.
4. There aren't some / any apples.
5. My mum has got some / any cakes.
6. Are there any / some eggs in the basket?
7. Is there some / any milk in the fridge?

 .... / 6 marks

B Write.

> behind   in   in front of   ~~next to~~   on   on   under

1. My friend sits ___next to___ me at school.
2. The teacher is _____ the class. She is talking to the pupils.
3. I'm sitting _____ my chair.
4. Don't put your feet _____ the table.
5. My books and pencils are _____ my bag.
6. I can't see my shoes. They're _____ the bed.
7. Don't look _____ you. Look at the teacher.

 .... / 6 marks

C Write Where is or Where are and match.

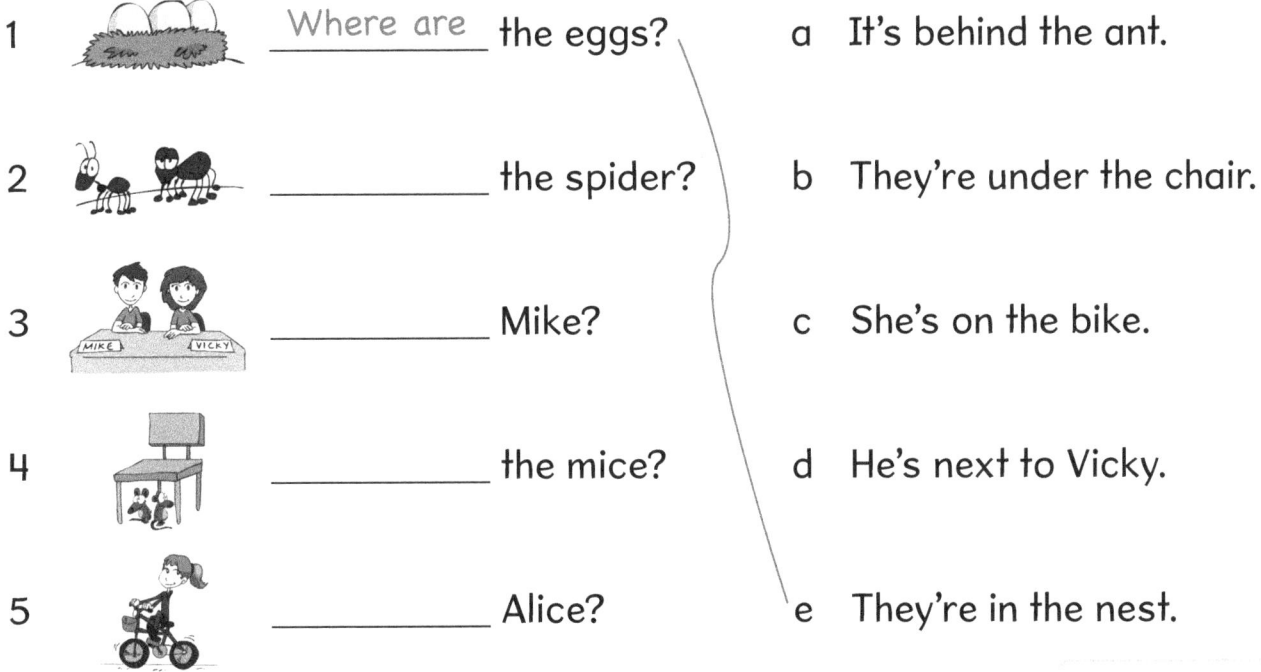

1. ___Where are___ the eggs?   a It's behind the ant.
2. _____ the spider?   b They're under the chair.
3. _____ Mike?   c She's on the bike.
4. _____ the mice?   d He's next to Vicky.
5. _____ Alice?   e They're in the nest.

 .... / 4 marks

Test 4

D Circle.

1. Elizabeth play / (plays) tennis on Mondays.
2. Bobby study / studies maths at the weekend.
3. John go / goes to the cinema on Sunday.
4. Mum and Dad watch / watches TV in the evening.
5. My brother and sister ride / rides their bikes at 6 o'clock.
6. I like / likes rollercoasters.
7. Pilots fly / flies aeroplanes.
8. Harry wear / wears funny clothes.

...... / 7 marks

E Write don't or doesn't.

1. Elephants ____don't____ eat meat.
2. Mr Robins _____ ride a bike.
3. Peter _____ drive.
4. Her sisters _____ like winter.
5. You _____ eat cakes.
6. I _____ live in Paris.

...... / 5 marks

F Write.

eat
~~get~~
go
go
have
ride

1. __Do__ Max and Tilly __get__ up at 7 o'clock?   Yes, they do.
2. _____ they _____ breakfast at 9 o'clock?   _____
3. _____ they _____ to school after breakfast?   _____
4. _____ they _____ sandwiches at 1 o'clock?   _____
5. _____ Max _____ his bike after school?   _____
6. _____ Tilly _____ to bed at 5 o' clock?   _____

...... / 5 marks

Test 4

G Write in, on or at.

1 Kyle eats breakfast ___in___ the morning.
2 My Dad gets up _____ 7 o'clock.
3 Mum cooks _____ Monday and Tuesday.
4 My sister does homework _____ Sunday.
5 I play tennis _____ the weekend.
6 I read a book _____ the evening.
7 Erik listens to music _____ night.
8 The boys watch DVDs _____ Saturdays.

_____ / 7 marks

H Match.

1 What does Mike do on Sunday?   a They brush their teeth.
2 What do the children do at night?   b He goes to the park.
3 What does Sally do in the evening?   c You go to school.
4 What do we do in the morning?   d We have breakfast.
5 What do you do at the weekend?   e I play with my friends.
6 What do I do at 8 o'clock?   f She watches TV.

_____ / 5 marks

I Circle.

1 What / (Where) are my socks?
2 What / Who is Sam watching?
3 Who / What is Scooby Doo?
4 Where / When is Eid?
5 What / Who is a rhinoceros?
6 When / Where is the zoo?

_____ / 5 marks

_____ / 50 marks

95

Happy Trails 1 Grammar Book
International Edition
Erika Antorka

Publisher: Jason Mann
Director of Content Development: Sarah Bideleux
Commissioning Editor: Carol Goodwright
Development Editor: Lynn Thomson
Assistant Editor: Manuela Barros
Content Project Editor: Amy Smith
Production Controller: Tom Relf
Art Director: Natasa Arsenidou
Cover Designer: Vasiliki Christoforidou
Text Designer: Vicky Hatzievangelinou
Compositor: Rouli Manias
National Geographic Editorial Liaison: Leila Hishmeh

Acknowledgments

Illustrated by Panagiotis Angeletakis,
George Melissaropoulos

The publisher would like to thank the following sources for permission to reproduce their copyright protected photos:

Cover: (left to right): National Geographic Image Collection – (Jim Richardson), (Dick Durrance II), (Jimmy Chin), (Fritz Hoffmann).

Inside: iStockphoto – p29 (S. Ugur Okcu); National Geographic Image Collection – pp. 23 (Sam Dobrow), 41 (Mattias Klum, George Grall), 49 (Steve Raymer); Thinkstock – pp47 (iStockphoto, iStockphoto). All other photos courtesy of Shutterstock.

© 2012 National Geographic Learning, as part of Cengage Learning

ALL RIGHTS RESERVED. No part of this work covered by the copyright herein may be reproduced, transmitted, stored, or used in any form or by any means graphic, electronic, or mechanical, including but not limited to photocopying, recording, scanning, digitizing, taping, Web distribution, information networks, or information storage and retrieval systems, except as permitted under Section 107 or 108 of the 1976 United States Copyright Act, without the prior written permission of the publisher.

For permission to use material from this text or product,
submit all requests online at **www.cengage.com/permissions**

Further permissions questions can be emailed to
permissionrequest@cengage.com

ISBN: 978-1-133-05013-1

National Geographic Learning
Cheriton House
North Way
Andover
Hampshire
SP10 5BE
United Kingdom

Cengage Learning is a leading provider of customized learning solutions with office locations around the globe, including Singapore, the United Kingdom, Australia, Mexico, Brazil and Japan. Locate your local office at:
international.cengage.com/region

Cengage Learning products are represented in Canada by Nelson Education, Ltd.

Visit National Geographic Learning online at **ngl.cengage.com**

Visit our corporate website at **www.cengage.com**

www.ingramcontent.com/pod-product-compliance
Ingram Content Group UK Ltd.
Pitfield, Milton Keynes, MK11 3LW, UK
UKHW060159240426
12048UKWH00028B/1662